P.180 ——— old girl write this out
P.198 Rainy Night in Georgia ✓
P.38
P.8?
P.54) P.9 Earth, W A F, ✓
P.88 — it a mean world (write this out)
P.115
P.157 Marty, Mercy Me
P.167 —
P.186
P.20?
P.218 ✓
P.222
P.240 — 242 ✓
P.246   )
P.250
P.23
P.110
P.?
P.???
P.???
P.??0
P.242 EARTH, WIND & FIRE
~~P.~~ Earth wind & fire .
P150 LOVE CHILD
P.26? what going ~~~~
214. Earth, W, F
~~232~~

AFTER THE LOVE HAS GONE

Words and Music by DAVID FOSTER,
JAY GRAYDON and BILL CHAMPLIN

BABY, WHAT YOU WANT ME TO DO

Words and Music by
JIMMY REED

10

AIN'T NOTHING LIKE THE REAL THING

Words and Music by NICKOLAS ASHFORD
and VALERIE SIMPSON

16

BUT IT'S ALRIGHT

Words and Music by JEROME L. JACKSON
and PIERRE TUBBS

You don't know   how   I   feel. ___   You'll
One ___ day   you'll   see ___   you'll
There's one thing   I   wan - na say,   you'll

nev - er know _____   how   I   feel. ___
nev - er find _____   a   guy   like   me
meet   a guy _____   who'll make you pay,

CAN'T GET ENOUGH OF YOUR LOVE, BABE

Words and Music by
BARRY WHITE

25

28

COLD SWEAT, PT. 1

Words and Music by JAMES BROWN
and ALFRED JAMES ELLIS

DANCING IN THE STREET

Words and Music by MARVIN GAYE,
IVY HUNTER and WILLIAM STEVENSON

37

EVERYBODY PLAYS THE FOOL, SOMETIME

Words and Music by RUDY CLARK,
KENNY WILLIAMS and JIM BAILEY

Not too fast

Ah.

Woh, _____ ah. _____

O - kay, _ so your heart _ is bro - ken. _

But there's no guar - an - tee____ that the one you love____ is gon-na love
and your a - bil - i - ty_____ to rea - son____ is swept a - way__

you. _____ Oh, _____ lov-ing eyes they can-not see,__ a
Oh, _____ heav-en on earth is ___ all you see,__ you're

cer-tain per - son could nev-er__ be. __ Love runs deep-er than an - y o - cean,
out of touch__ with re - al - i - ty.__ And now you cry____ but when you do __

clouds your mind with __ e - mo - tion. _____
next time a - round some-one __ cries for

FINGERTIPS (PART 2)

Words and Music by CLARENCE O. PAUL
and HENRY COSBY

47

48

Solo ends I know that I nev-er gon-na hey, yeah.__ Ev-'ry-

bod - y had a good time. __ So if you want me to, if you want me to; I'm gon-na

swing this song, __ yeah, just a one more time __ un - til I come back, __

__ just a one more time __ when I come back. __ So be ad - vised. *Harmonica solo*

Cm

GET UP
(I Feel Like Being)
A SEX MACHINE

Words and Music by JAMES BROWN,
BOBBY BYRD and RONALD LENHOFF

Shout: Fellas, I'm ready to get up and do my thing,
I wanta get into it, man, you know ...
Like a, like a sex machine, man,
Movin' ... doin' it, you know
Can I count it off? (Go ahead)

(E♭7)
use your form
Stay on the scene like a
sex ma - chine.
You got to have the feel - ing
sure as you're born
Get it to - geth - er
right on, right on.

ADDITIONAL WORDS

I said the feeling you got to get,
Give me the fever in a cold sweat.
The way I like it is the way it is;
I got mine and don't worry 'bout his.

Get on up and then shake your money maker,
Shake your money maker, etc.

GOT TO GIVE IT UP

Words and Music by
MARVIN GAYE

56

3. Move your body, move baby, and dance all night,
   To the groovin', I feel all right.
   Havin' a party, ooh, invite all your friends;
   But if you see me stop by, let me in.
   Baby, just party all night long.
   Let me slip into your erotic zone.
   (We heard that!)

   (Extra Lyrics for Ad Lib Ending)
   Keep on dancin', oh keep on dancin'.
   Ooh, look so good, yeah, keep on dancin'.
   Oh, now sugar, got to give it up.
   Keep on dancin', gotta give it up.
   Keep on dancin' . . . .

GRAZING IN THE GRASS

Words by HARRY ELSTON
Music by PHILEMON HOU

62

HEATWAVE
(Love Is Like a Heatwave)

Words and Music by EDWARD HOLLAND,
LAMONT DOZIER and BRIAN HOLLAND

I CAN'T STOP LOVING YOU

Words and Music by
DON GIBSON

I CAN'T GET NEXT TO YOU

Words and Music by BARRETT STRONG
and NORMAN WHITFIELD

can't get next to you＿ babe,   I   can't get next to you.＿

can't   get   next   to   you,＿   I

can't get next to you＿ babe,   I   can't get next to you.＿

Guitar solo
(at pitch)

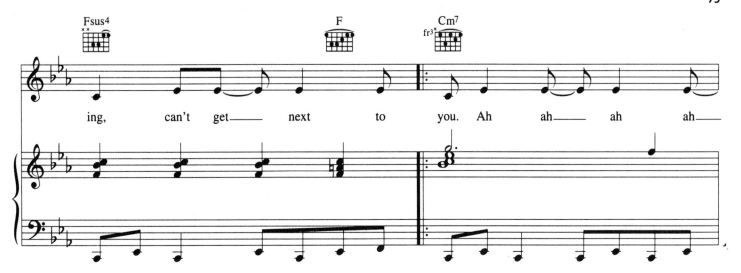

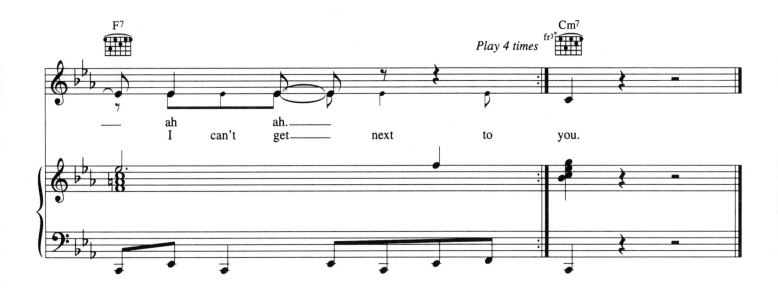

Verse 2:
I can fly like a bird in the sky
And I can buy anything that money can buy.
I can turn a river into a raging fire
I can live forever if I so desire.
I don't want it, all these things I can do
'Cause I can't get next to you.

Verse 3:
I can turn back the hands of time - you better believe I can
I can make the seasons change just by waving my hand.
I can change anything from old to new
The thing I want to do the most I'm unable to do.
I'm an unhappy woman with all the powers I possess
'Cause man, you're the key to my happiness.

I GOT THE FEELIN'

Words and Music by
JAMES BROWN

I GOT YOU
(I Feel Good)

Words and Music by
JAMES BROWN

82

I HEARD IT THROUGH THE GRAPEVINE

Words and Music by NORMAN J. WHITFIELD
and BARRETT STRONG

I SECOND THAT EMOTION

Words and Music by WILLIAM "SMOKEY" ROBINSON
and ALFRED CLEVELAND

I WANT YOU BACK

Words and Music by FREDDIE PERREN, ALPHONSO MIZELL,
BERRY GORDY and DEKE RICHARDS

I'LL BE THERE

Words and Music by BERRY GORDY, HAL DAVIS,
WILLIE HUTCH and BOB WEST

I'M LOSING YOU
(I Know)

Words and Music by CORNELIUS GRANT,
NORMAN WHITFIELD and EDWARD HOLLAND

Your love ___ is fad - in', I can

IF I WERE YOUR WOMAN

Words and Music by LAVERNE WARE,
PAM SAWYER and CLAY McMURRAY

IT'S A MAN'S MAN'S MAN'S WORLD

Words and Music by JAMES BROWN
and BETTY NEWSOME

Additional Lyrics

Man thinks about the little bitty baby girls and the baby boys.
Man makes them happy 'cause man makes them toys.
And after man makes everything, everything he can
You know that man makes money to buy from other men.
This is a man's world, but it wouldn't be nothing
Without a woman or a girl.

IT'S YOUR THING

Words and Music by RUDOLPH ISLEY, RONALD ISLEY
and O'KELLY ISLEY

To Coda ⊕

JUST ONCE

Words by CYNTHIA WEIL
Music by BARRY MANN

LADY MARMALADE

Words and Music by BOB CREWE
and KENNY NOLAN

Moderate groove

(Hey sis- ter, go sis- ter,

soul sis- ter, go sis- ter. Hey sis- ter, go sis- ter, soul sis- ter, go sis- ter.) He

met Mar- ma- lade __ down in old __ New Or- leans, __ strut- tin' her stuff __ on the street. __

black sat-in sheets, I swear __ he start-ed to freak. __

Hey, __ hey, __ hey __

LET'S GET IT ON

Words and Music by MARVIN GAYE
and ED TOWNSEND

Slow Soul beat

I've been real-ly try - in', ba-by, try-in' to hold _ back this feel-

in' for so _ long. And if you feel like _ I feel, _ ba-by,

then come on, _ on, _ come on. Ooh, _ let's get it on. Ow, _

140

141

LIVING FOR THE CITY

Words and Music by
STEVIE WONDER

Original key: Gb major. This edition has been transposed up one half-step to be more playable.

LONELY TEARDROPS

Words and Music by BERRY GORDY,
GWEN GORDY FUQUA and TYRAN CARLO

Moderato, Not Too Fast, With A Beat

LOVE CHILD

Words and Music by DEKE RICHARDS,
PAMELA SAWYER, DEAN R. TAYLOR
and FRANK E. WILSON

MERCY, MERCY ME
(The Ecology)

Words and Music by
MARVIN GAYE

MUSTANG SALLY

Words and Music by
BONNY RICE

Moderate Blues Rock

Mus - tang   Sal - ly.

Think you bet - ter slow your   mus - tang   down.

Mus - tang

OOO BABY BABY

Words and Music by WILLIAM "SMOKEY" ROBINSON
and WARREN MOORE

Lyrics:

Ooo, la, la, la, la, I did you _ wrong; _ my heart _ went out to
takes, _ I know _ I've made a

play, and in the game, _ I lost you. _ What a price to
few, but I'm on-ly hu-man; _ you've made mis-takes

pay! _ I'm cry-in'. Ooo, _ ba-by
too! _

(You Make Me Feel Like)
A NATURAL WOMAN

Words and Music by GERRY GOFFIN,
CAROLE KING and JERRY WEXLER

172

NOWHERE TO RUN

Words and Music by LAMONT DOZIER,
BRIAN HOLLAND and EDDIE HOLLAND

OH GIRL

Words and Music by
EUGENE RECORD

Oh, _____ girl, _____

C#m

I guess I bet-ter go. ___ I can save my-self ___ a lot of use-less tears. ___

D

Bm   D/E   A

Girl, I've got ___ to get a-way from here. ___ Oh, _____ girl, ___ pain will

C#m

dou-ble if you leave me now ___ 'cause I don't know where ___ to look for love, ___

D

PAIN IN MY HEART

Moderate Blues Ballad

Words and Music by
NAOMI NEVILLE

PAPA'S GOT A BRAND NEW BAG

Words and Music by
JAMES BROWN

PAPA WAS A ROLLIN' STONE

Words and Music by NORMAN WHITFIELD
and BARRETT STRONG

It was the third of Sep-tem-ber.

nev-er got a chance to see ___

That day I'll al-ways re-mem-ber, yes I will, ___ 'cause

___ him. Nev-er heard noth-in' but bad things a-bout him.

A RAINY NIGHT IN GEORGIA

Words and Music by
TONY JOE WHITE

Moderately

Ebmaj7   Dbmaj7   Ebmaj7

Ebmaj7   Ab

1. Hov-erin' by my suit-case, ___ tryin' to find a warm place to
2. Ne-on signs a-flash-in', ___ tax-i cabs and busses pass-in'
3. *(See additional lyrics)*

Ebmaj7

spend the night;
through the night;

A heav-y rain a fall-in';
The dis-tant moan-in' of a train

Ab   Ebmaj7

Seems I hear your voice call-in' "It's all right."
Seems to play a sad re-frain to the night;

Additional Lyrics

3. I find me a place in a box car,
   So I take out my guitar to pass some time;
   Late at night when it's hard to rest,
   I hold your picture to my chest, and I'm all right;
   (To Chorus)

SEXUAL HEALING

Words and Music by MARVIN GAYE,
ODELL BROWN and DAVID RITZ

208

Let's make love to-night!___ Wake up, wake up,

wake up, wake up, 'cause you do it right!___

Repeat and Fade

SAY IT LOUD
(I'm Black and I'm Proud)

Words and Music by JAMES BROWN
and ALFRED JAMES ELLIS

See Spoken lyrics:

Repeat as needed

D.S. and Fade
(with repeats)

Rap Lyrics

Verse 1:
Say it loud: "I'm black and I'm proud."
Say it loud: "I'm black and I'm proud."
Some people say we got a lot of malice,
Some say it's a lot of nerve
But I say we won't quit moving until we get what we deserve.
We've been 'buked and we've been scorned,
We've been treated bad, talked about as sure as you're born.
But just as sure as it takes two eyes to make a pair.
Brother we can't quit until we get our share.
Say it loud: "I'm black and I'm proud."
Say it loud: "I'm black and I'm proud."
Say it loud: "I'm black and I'm proud."
I've worked on jobs with my feet and my hands,
But all that work I did was for the other man.
Now we demand a chance to do things for ourselves.
We're tired of beating our head against the wall
And working for someone else.
Say it loud: "I'm black and I'm proud." (4 times)

Bridge:
Ooh-ee, you're killing me.
Alright, you're outa sight.
Alright, so tough, you're tough enough.
Ooh-ee, you're killing me.

Verse 2:
Say it loud: "I'm black and I'm proud."
Say it loud: "I'm black and I'm proud."
Now we demand a chance to do things for ourselves. We're tired of beating
our heads against the wall
And working for someone else.
We're people, we're like the birds and the bees,
But we'd rather die on our feet than keep living on our knees.
Say it loud: "I'm black and I'm proud." (3 times)

Fade on Bridge

SEPTEMBER

Words and Music by MAURICE WHITE,
AL McKAY and ALLEE WILLIS

Moderate Rock

Do you re - mem-ber the twen - ty - first night___ of Sep -
ring - ing in the key___ that our souls___ were___ sing -

tem - ber? Love was chang-ing the mind's___ pre - ten - ders while___
ing as we danced in the night.___ Re - mem - ber how the

216

Ba - de - ya,— danc - ing in Sep - tem - ber, ba - de - ya,—

{ nev - er was a cloud - y day._____
{ gold - en dreams were shin - y days._____

Repeat and fade

3rd Verse

My thoughts are with you,
holding hands with your heart,
to see you, only blue talk and love.
Remember how we knew love was here to stay?

4th Verse

Now December found the love that we shared,
September, only blue talk and love.
Remember the true love we share today.

SHINING STAR

Words and Music by MAURICE WHITE,
PHILIP BAILEY and LARRY DUNN

SIGNED, SEALED, DELIVERED I'M YOURS

Words and Music by STEVIE WONDER, SYREETA WRIGHT,
LEE GARRETT and LULA MAE HARDAWAY

THINK

Words and Music by
LOWMAN PAULING

Rock beat

D7

(Think,)
(think,)
(think) a-bout the good things.   (Think,)

a-bout the bad   things.___   a-bout the right things.
(think)   (Think,)   (think)   (Think,)

A7   G7

a-bout the wrong things. Now, la-dy be-fore_ you leave me   re-al-ize___ that I'm the
(think)

SIR DUKE

Words and Music by
STEVIE WONDER

Mu - sic is a world with - in it - self _____ with a
Mu - sic knows it is and al - ways will _____ be one of

lan - guage we all un - der - stand, _____
the things that life just won't quit. _____

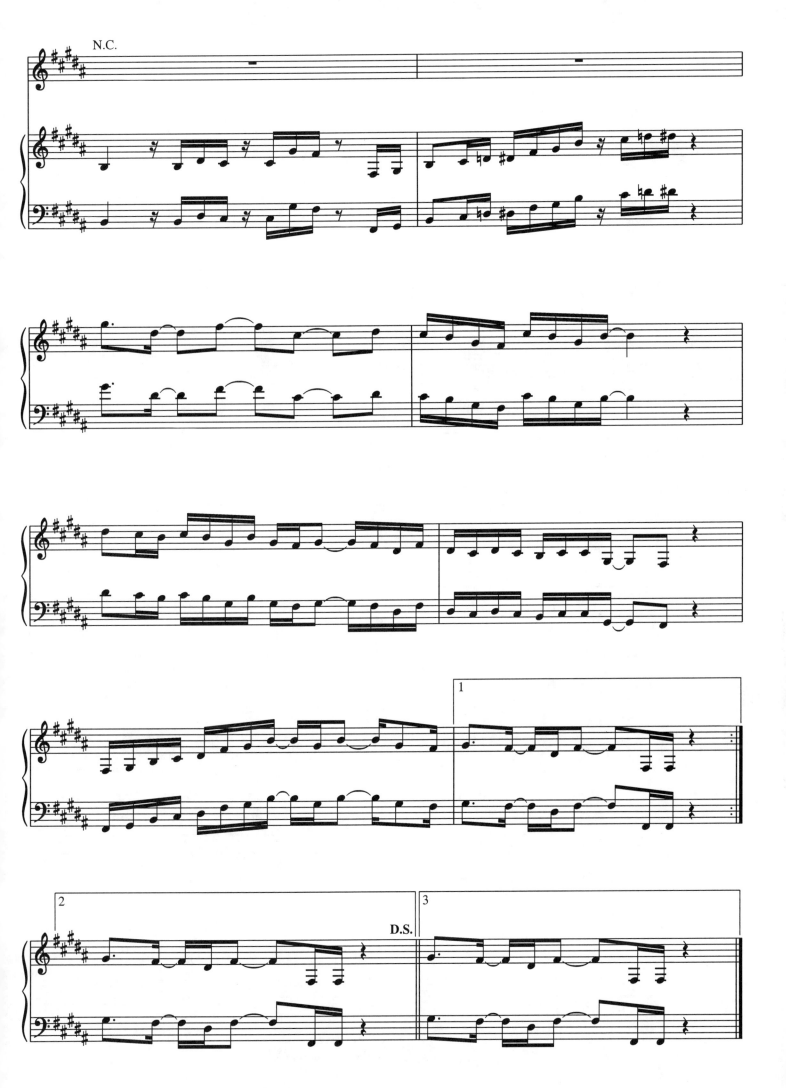

SMILING FACES SOMETIMES

Words and Music by NORMAN WHITFIELD
and BARRETT STRONG

234

SUPERSTITION

Words and Music by
STEVIE WONDER

TELL IT LIKE IT IS

Words and Music by GEORGE DAVIS
and LEE DIAMOND

THAT'S THE WAY OF THE WORLD

Words and Music by MAURICE WHITE,
CHARLES STEPNEY and VERDINE WHITE

THIS WILL BE
(An Everlasting Love)

Words and Music by MARVIN YANCY
and CHUCK JACKSON

248

TOO BUSY THINKING
ABOUT MY BABY

Words and Music by JANIE BRADFORD,
NORMAN WHITFIELD and BARRETT STRONG

grow, _____ ain't _____ nev - er give it a thought _____ to

where riv - ers flow. _____

Ain't got time _____ for noth - in' else.

I ain't got time _____ to dis - cuss the weath - er, or know _____ what's go - ing

THE TRACKS OF MY TEARS

Words and Music by WILLIAM "SMOKEY" ROBINSON,
WARREN MOORE and MARVIN TARPLIN

Do, do, do, ___ doot. Do, do, do, ___ doot. Do, do, do, ___

___ doot. Do, do, do, do, do, do. ___

Peo - ple say I'm the
Since you left me, if you

life of the par - ty 'cause ___ I tell a joke or two. ___ Al-though I
see me with an - oth - er girl, seem - in' like I'm hav - in' fun. ___ Al-though she

255

UPTIGHT
(Everything's Alright)

Words and Music by STEVIE WONDER,
SYLVIA MOY and HENRY COSBY

Ba - by, ev - 'ry-thing is all right, up - tight, out __ of sight. __

Ba - by, ev - 'ry-thing is all right, up - tight, out __ of sight. __ I'm a

poor man's son __ from a-cross the rail-road tracks. __ The on - ly shirt I own __ is hang -
no one __ is bet - ter than I. I know I'm __ just an __

THE WAY YOU DO THE THINGS YOU DO

Words and Music by WILLIAM "SMOKEY" ROBINSON
and ROBERT ROGERS

WHAT'S GOING ON

Words and Music by MARVIN GAYE,
AL CLEVELAND and RENALDO BENSON

YOU'VE REALLY GOT A HOLD ON ME

Words and Music by
WILLIAM "SMOKEY" ROBINSON

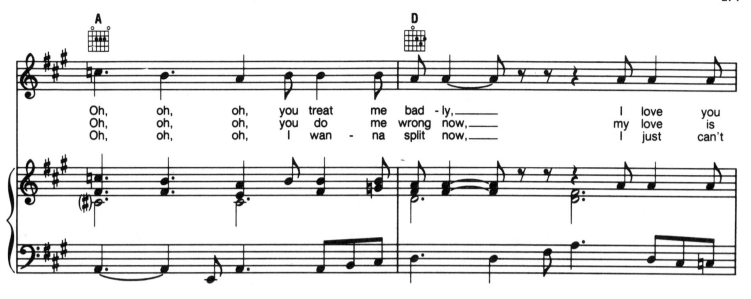

Oh, oh, oh, you treat me bad - ly,_____ I love you
Oh, oh, oh, you do me wrong now,_____ my love you is
Oh, oh, oh, I wan - na split now,_____ I just can't

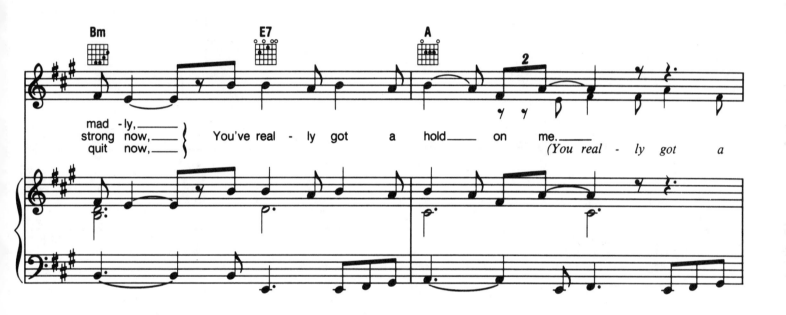

mad - ly,_____
strong now,_____ } You've real - ly got a hold_____ on me._____
quit now,_____ *(You real - ly got a*

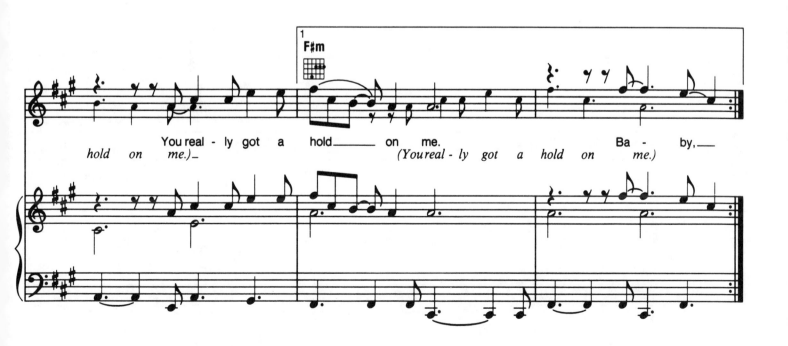

You real - ly got a hold_____ on me. Ba - by,___
*hold on me.)_* *(You real - ly got a hold on me.)*

(Your Love Keeps Lifting Me)
HIGHER AND HIGHER

Words and Music by GARY JACKSON,
CARL SMITH and RAYNARD MINER

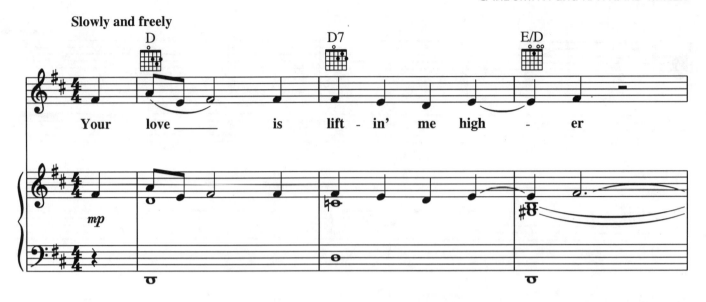

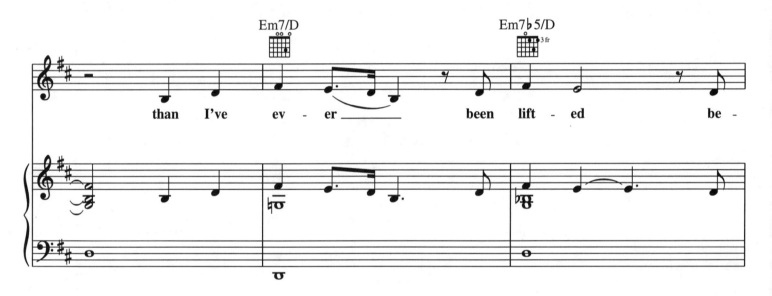

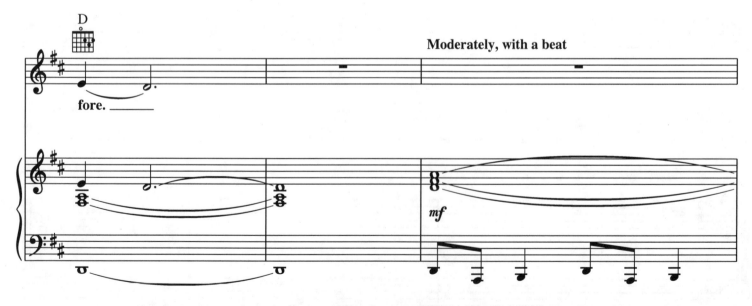

WAR

Words and Music by NORMAN WHITFIELD
and BARRETT STRONG

Slow Rock (with double time feel)

1. War,   Uh!   What is it
2.,3. (See additional lyrics)

good _ for?_ Ab - so - lute - ly noth-ing.   War,   Uh!

What is it good __ for? _____ Ab - so - lute - ly

War means tears — in thou - sands of mo-thers' eyes — when their

Fade on last repeat

sons go out to fight _ and lose _ their _____ lives. _ I said

Additional Lyrics

2. War, uh! What is it good for? Absolutely nothing; say it again;
War, uh! What is it good for? Absolutely nothing.
War, it's nothing but a heartbreaker; War, friend only to the undertaker.
War is an enemy to all mankind. The thought of war blows my mind.
War has caused unrest within the younger generation;
Induction then destruction, who wants to die? Ah
War, uh um; What is it good for? You tell me nothing, um!
War, uh! What is it good for? Absolutely nothing.
Good God, war, it's nothing but a heartbreaker;
War, friend only to the undertaker;

3. Wars have shattered many a young man's dreams;
Made him disabled, bitter and mean.
Life is much too short and precious to spend fighting wars each day.
War can't give life, it can only take it away. Ah
War, Uh um! What is it good for? Absolutely nothing, um.
War, good God almighty, listen, what is it good for? Absolutely nothing, yeah.
War, it's nothing but a heartbreaker; War, friend only to the undertaker.
Peace, love and understanding, tell me is there no place for them today?
They say we must fight to keep our freedom, but Lord knows it's gotta be a better way.
I say war, uh um, yeah, yeah. What is it good for? Absolutely nothing; say it again;
War, yea, yea, yea, yea, what is it good for? Absolutely nothing; say it again;
War, nothing but a heartbreaker; What is it good for? Friend only to the undertaker.....
(Fade)